# Introduction

Welcome to "250 Life Hacks" your indispensable companion to navigating the delightful chaos of daily life with a smile. In this unique guide, we delve into the universal qu minor predicaments we ingenious solutions i dose of

Each chapter in this book tackles a different aspect of life, from the mundane to the unexpected. Whether it's mastering the art of work-life balance, outsmarting the capriciousness of technology, or handling the unpredictable whims of Mother Nature, we've got you covered with practical tips, clever tricks, and a generous sprinkling of laughter.

So, are you ready to transform everyday challenges into moments of triumph and giggles? Let's dive in!

# Table of Contents

- Shopping and Consumerism
- Shopping and Consumerism
- Communication and Media
- Construction and DIY Projects
- Psychology and Behavior
- Nature and Environment
- Fashion and Personal Care
- Safety and Security
- Art and Creativity
- Time Management and Procrastination
- Social Media and Internet Culture
- Philosophy and Ethics
- For Teens
- For Women
- For Men
- For Seniors

# CHRISTMAS

"Anything that can go wrong,
will go wrong."

## The "easy-to-open" package won't be.

 **Have scissors or a box cutter handy.**

# CHRISTMAS

**Your Christmas lights will work perfectly during the test run but fail as soon as guests arrive.**

**Have a backup set of lights and check the fuses beforehand.**

**The ornament you cherish the most will be the first to break.**

**Keep fragile ornaments higher up on the tree, away from kids and pets.**

# CHRISTMAS

**The perfect gift you've planned for months will go on sale the day after Christmas.** SALE

 **Keep receipts and be aware of post-holiday sales policies.**

**The one year you skip making extra gravy is the year everyone wants it.**

 **Always make more gravy than you think you need.**

**The batteries for the new toys will be the one size you don't have.**

 **Stock up on various types of batteries before the holidays.**

**Your relatives will arrive early when you're least prepared and late when the meal is time-sensitive.**

 **Plan for flexibility and have some appetizers ready.**

# CHRISTMAS

The year you decide to go "all out" with decorations is the year your neighbor outdoes you.

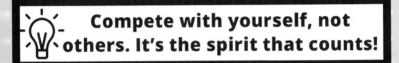

Compete with yourself, not others. It's the spirit that counts!

You'll remember you forgot to buy wrapping paper when you're wrapping presents late on Christmas Eve.

Stock up on gift bags and tissue paper as emergency backups.

# CHRISTMAS

The Christmas recipe you decide to try for the first time will not turn out as expected.

 Have a tried-and-true dish as a backup.

The more effort you put into hiding gifts, the more likely your family is to stumble upon them.

 Consider keeping gifts at a trustworthy friend's house until the big day.

# CHRISTMAS

The one Christmas movie everyone agrees on watching will not be available on any of your streaming services.

 Plan some alternatives or consider renting the movie online.

You'll buy enough food to feed an army, but the one thing everyone craves will run out first.

 Try to gauge the crowd's favorite foods in advance, and stock up accordingly.

# CHRISTMAS

The more intricate the toy, the harder it will be to assemble, especially late at night on Christmas Eve.

 Read assembly instructions in advance and make sure you have all the necessary tools.

No matter how early you send Christmas cards, you'll receive one from someone you forgot to include on your list.

 Have a few extra generic cards and gifts on hand for unexpected exchanges.

# CHRISTMAS

The uglier the Christmas sweater, the more likely you are to win the contest.

 If you're aiming to win, go for shock value.

You'll remember a crucial ingredient missing in your Christmas dinner recipe only when all stores are closed.

 Double-check your shopping list and pantry, and consider buying extra staple items.

# CHRISTMAS

You'll remember where you hid last year's Christmas presents after you've bought new ones for this year.

 Keep a designated "gift closet" so you don't lose track of your presents.

The amount of tape you have will be inversely proportional to the amount of wrapping you need to do.

 Always buy an extra roll of tape; you'll use it eventually.

# TECHNOLOGY AND COMPUTERS

Your computer will only crash when you haven't saved your work.

 Save your work so frequently that it becomes your new nervous tic.

Wi-Fi signals obey the inverse square law: the closer you are to needing it, the weaker it gets.

 Use a Wi-Fi extender or, better yet, use an old-fashioned Ethernet cable.

# TECHNOLOGY AND COMPUTERS

**Your most embarrassing typos will always autocorrect into something even more embarrassing.**

**Re-read messages, especially to your boss and your crush, unless you want to explain why you wrote "duck" or "shirt."**

* * * * *

**Your printer will have enough ink for tests but run out when printing important documents.**

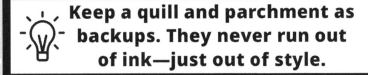 **Keep a quill and parchment as backups. They never run out of ink—just out of style.**

* * * * *

# TECHNOLOGY AND COMPUTERS

**Your favorite software will update and lose all the features you actually use.**

**Stick to pencil and paper; they haven't had an annoying update yet.**

**When you finally remember your password, the system will ask you to change it.**

**Use forgettable milestones as your new passwords. For example, "ForgotMyAnniversaryAgain!"**

# WORK AND OFFICE LIFE

**The more crucial the email, the more likely it will land in your spam folder**

Regularly check your spam folder or risk missing out on that "urgent" memo about Casual Friday.

# WORK AND OFFICE LIFE

The less you're qualified for a meeting, the more likely you are to be called into it.

 Carry around a stack of papers; it makes you look busy and possibly immune to useless meetings ;)

The likelihood of your boss walking in is directly proportional to how much fun you're having.

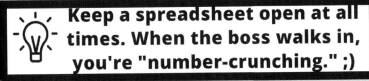 Keep a spreadsheet open at all times. When the boss walks in, you're "number-crunching." ;)

The one day you sleep in is the one day the boss comes in early.

Have a work friend text you if they spot the boss coming in early. Return the favor.

The easier the task, the harder it is to explain why it took so long.

Become adept at using jargon. "I was synergizing the cross-functional deliverables" sounds better than "I was doing almost nothing."

# WORK AND OFFICE LIFE

The coffee will run out as soon as you get to the front of the line.

 Befriend the person in charge of the coffee. That's power.

If you nail the presentation, your PowerPoint will fail.

 Have a backup plan: interpretive dance.

# HOME AND HOUSEHOLD

The missing sock reappears only after its partner has been thrown away.

 Consider sock puppetry as a new hobby.

# HOME AND HOUSEHOLD

The tool or ingredient you need will be at the back of the deepest drawer or cabinet.
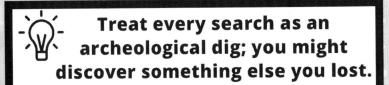

Treat every search as an archeological dig; you might discover something else you lost.

The more you clean, the more likely your child will immediately make a mess.

 Invest in disposable furniture, or just cover everything in plastic.

# HOME AND HOUSEHOLD

Your neighbors will decide to mow their lawn the moment you sit down to relax.

 Always have noise-cancelling headphones within arm's reach.

* * * * *

The Wi-Fi will go down the moment you start streaming your favorite show.

 Use this as an opportunity to read or—let's be real—panic.

* * * * *

# HOME AND HOUSEHOLD

You'll remember you forgot to take out the trash just as the garbage truck drives away.

Make friends with the garbage collector. Sometimes human connection can save you from a week of stink.

* * * * *

* * * * *

# ☀ TRANSPORTATION AND TRAVEL ☀

The faster lane in traffic will slow down the moment you switch to it.

 Consider installing a revolving chair in your car so you can at least spin while you sulk.

Your flight will only be on time when you're running late.

 Always run late; it seems to be good luck.

# *TRANSPORTATION AND TRAVEL

The nearest gas station is inversely proportional to how desperately you need one.

 Keep an empty gas can and a sense of adventure in the trunk.

Your luggage will show up on the carousel after everyone else's, especially if you're in a hurry.

Make your luggage so ugly, no one would dare take it before you do.

# TRANSPORTATION AND TRAVEL

The person seated next to you will either talk too much or snore too loudly.

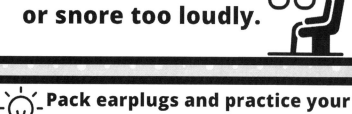

 Pack earplugs and practice your "I'm not interested" face.

The scenic route will become the lost route.

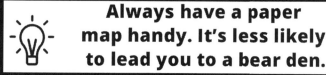 Always have a paper map handy. It's less likely to lead you to a bear den.

# TRANSPORTATION AND TRAVEL

When you don't need a restroom, you'll see one every mile. When you do, they'll all be closed for cleaning.

 Learn to appreciate the great outdoors or carry a "Closed for Cleaning" sign for emergencies.

# RELATIONSHIPS AND DATING

The one time you go out looking like a mess is the one time you'll run into your ex.

 Always wear sunglasses and a hat. You're not incognito; you're just fashionably mysterious.

You'll find the "perfect" match immediately after declaring a dating hiatus

 Declare a dating hiatus more often; it's apparently a good luck charm.

# RELATIONSHIPS AND DATING

The harder you try to impress someone, the more likely you'll embarrass yourself.

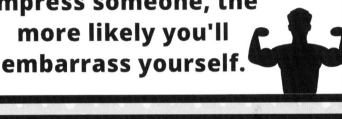

Lower expectations by sharing your most embarrassing story up front.

The relationship will get serious precisely when your free trial on the dating app expires.

Keep a backup of free dating apps; you never know when you'll need to circle back.

# RELATIONSHIPS AND DATING

Your date will order the most garlic-filled dish on the menu if you're hoping for a kiss.

 Carry mints; they're like Cupid's little helpers.

The more desperate you are to make plans, the busier everyone else seems to be.

 Cultivate an air of mystery; don't respond to texts for at least 37 minutes.

# RELATIONSHIPS AND DATING

Your message will have a glaring typo only after you've hit "send" to someone you're trying to impress.

 Pretend it was a test to see if they're detail-oriented. If they correct you, they pass!

# PARENTING AND CHILDCARE

Your child will only need urgent attention when you're on an important call.

 Use your mute button judiciously and perfect the art of multi-tasking.

A child's desire to nap is inversely related to how tired the parent is.

 Invest in a good coffee maker; you're going to need it.

# PARENTING AND CHILDCARE

The toy you spent hours assembling will be less interesting than the box it came in.

 Save money by giving cardboard boxes as gifts.

Your child will remember they need a costume the day before the school play.

Keep a box of generic costumes. You never know when you'll need to whip out a pirate or a dinosaur.

# PARENTING AND CHILDCARE

The louder you whisper, the louder your child will talk.

 Learn basic sign language or charades; it's quieter and more entertaining.

You will always discover you're out of wipes at the most inconvenient time.

 Store emergency wipes everywhere.
And we mean everywhere.

# PARENTING AND CHILDCARE

**The more eager you are for your child to sleep in, the earlier they will wake up.**

 **Get a white noise machine. For you, not the child. They're already awake.**

# HEALTH AND MEDICINE

The itch you can't reach is always in the middle of your back.

 Keep a back scratcher in every room. They make excellent décor.

The prescription you need will be the one that's out of stock.

 Make friends with your pharmacist; maybe they'll tip you off to secret stock.

# HEALTH AND MEDICINE

**Your doctor will be running late only on the days you're in a rush.**

 **Bring a book. Or better yet, write your own Murphy's Laws while you wait.**

**The minute you say you feel better, you'll sneeze.**

**Never declare wellness; you're just tempting fate.**

# HEALTH AND MEDICINE

You'll remember you're supposed to fast for a test after a large breakfast.

 Put a Post-It on your coffee maker the night before. No coffee = no breakfast.

The gym is always busiest when you finally decide to go.

 Try reverse psychology. If you never plan to go, maybe it'll always be empty.

# HEALTH AND MEDICINE

**You'll find out about a recall on a product after you've just used it.**

 **Always have a sense of humor and an emergency contact.**

# FOOD AND COOKING

The recipe you're eager to try will require one ingredient you don't have.

 Master the art of substitution or keep a spice rack that rivals a grocery store.

Your smoke alarm doubles as a cooking timer.

 Treat it as applause for your "smokin'" culinary skills.

# FOOD AND COOKING

Your cake will
stick to the pan
when baking
for guests.

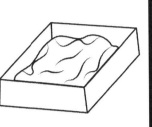

 Call it "deconstructed" and
claim it's avant-garde.

The '5-second rule'
turns into a 'no-second
rule' when you drop
your last piece of
chocolate.

 Keep a backup stash. Some
emergencies are chocolate
emergencies.

# FOOD AND COOKING

**Your blender will only malfunction when you've filled it with colored liquids.**

 Keep a mop handy; it's now part of your kitchen toolkit.

**The microwave will cook unevenly, leaving your food scorching hot and icy cold simultaneously.**

 Invest in microwave-safe plates that can also hold ice packs.

You'll realize you forgot to preheat the oven after you've prepared the mix.

 Use the waiting time to Instagram your #CookingFail and gather sympathy likes.

# WEATHER AND CLIMATE

The day you forget your umbrella is the day it will pour.

 Turn a grocery bag into an emergency rain hat. Chic and sustainable!

Your sunny vacation days will be forecasted with rain.

Always have a rainy-day activity on standby, like indoor skydiving or snorkeling in your bathtub.

# WEATHER AND CLIMATE

It will only snow after you've put away your winter gear.

Keep a single glove and hat handy; asymmetry is in fashion.

The wind will shift directions as soon as you start your barbecue.

Place your grill near a wall. Bonus: it can double as a smoke signal.

# WEATHER AND CLIMATE

**The weekend will be beautiful, but you'll be stuck indoors working.**

 **Set up a hammock in your living room and pretend you're on a beach.**

**The AC will break on the hottest day of the year.**

 **Fill a spray bottle with water and mist yourself while fanning with your utility bill.**

**You'll realize your car windows are down just as the rain starts.**

**Keep a chamois cloth in the glove box. You'll thank yourself later.**

# SPORTS AND FITNESS

The treadmill next to you will always be taken by the most enthusiastic exerciser.

 Use their energy as a source of motivation—or envy.
Your choice.

You'll finally make that three-pointer when no one is looking.

 Always carry confetti in your pocket for self-celebration.

# SPORTS AND FITNESS

Your yoga pants will rip only during the most compromising poses.

 Make "wardrobe malfunctions" a part of your routine. Own it.

The gym will schedule maintenance during your newfound commitment to fitness.

 Consider home workouts. Your living room rug makes a great yoga mat.

# SPORTS AND FITNESS

**Your earphones will tangle at the exact moment you're ready for a run.**

 **Use the untangling time to stretch. You were probably going to skip it anyway.**

**Your favorite sports team will only lose when you're watching.**

 **Record the game. Either you get to fast-forward through the misery or relive the glory.**

# SPORTS AND FITNESS

**The water fountain will be out of order after your most grueling workout.**

 **Always bring your own water, and maybe an emergency slice of lemon for flavor.**

# EDUCATION AND LEARNING

**The answer comes to you the moment after you hand in the test.**

**Always bring an eraser; you'll never know when enlightenment will strike.**

**Your laptop will update and restart during the most critical part of your online lecture.**

**Keep a notepad and pen as backup. Old school is still cool.**

# EDUCATION AND LEARNING

The simplest math problem will become impossible when someone's watching you solve it.

💡 Pretend you're in a math music video. Dramatize the struggle for comedic effect.

* * * * *

The book you need for your research will be checked out of the library.

💡 Befriend the librarian. They're the real keepers of knowledge.

# EDUCATION AND LEARNING

## You will only understand the material after the semester is over.

 Frame your 'aha' moment as "early preparation" for the next level.

## Your pen will run out of ink during the most important note-taking.

 Always carry a spare. Or two. Or three.

# EDUCATION AND LEARNING

**Your noisy classmates will be quiet, except during your moments of deep concentration.**

 **Noise-cancelling headphones are your friend, but earplugs are cheaper.**

# GOVERNMENT AND POLITICS

The politician you dislike the most will have the longest career.

 Take up meditation; you're going to need it.

Your chosen candidate will only start making gaffes after you've voted for them.

 Always keep a "told you so" in your pocket for your friends who voted the other way.

# GOVERNMENT AND POLITICS

Important legislation will always be decided while you're asleep.

 Set an alarm for ungodly hours. You can't be disappointed if you're not surprised.

Tax season will be at its most complicated when you're least prepared.

 Befriend an accountant. Or marry one, for permanent tax relief.

# GOVERNMENT AND POLITICS

**Political debates will turn into comedy skits when you want serious answers.**

 Watch debates with a bag of popcorn. Entertainment guaranteed.

**Your most political friend will only post their rants when you're trying to avoid politics.**

 Social media 'mute' buttons are there for a reason.

**The document you need at the DMV is the one you left at home.**

**Always carry a briefcase of every important document you've ever received.**

# FINANCES AND MONEY

You'll finally remember your budget the day after a shopping spree.

 Carry a pocket-sized budget guide; consult before every impulse buy.

Your credit card will decline on a first date at the fanciest restaurant.

 Always have an emergency $20 bill tucked in your shoe. It's your "sole-mate."

# FINANCES AND MONEY

You'll get an incredible job offer right after you've committed to another one.

 Network with everyone; you never know when you'll want to make a switch.

The stock you didn't invest in will skyrocket.

 Invest emotional stock in being "a good person," not just a wealthy one.

# FINANCES AND MONEY

**Unexpected expenses will appear just as you think you're saving money.**

 **Create a "Surprise Expenses" fund. It won't be a surprise anymore!**

**The ATM will be out of order when you're in dire need of cash.**

**Keep a stash of emergency money, but not under your mattress - that's the first place they look.**

# FINANCES AND MONEY

**You'll finally understand cryptocurrency when it's no longer a thing.**

 **Stick to what you know, but read up on what you don't. Ignorance is expensive.**

# ENTERTAINMENT AND LEISURE

The best part of the movie will be interrupted by a restroom emergency.

 Learn the art of the "bladder schedule" to sync with movie times.

Your favorite TV show will be canceled after a cliffhanger season finale.

 Always have a backup show in your queue; binge-therapy is real.

# ENTERTAINMENT AND LEISURE

## The game will lag only when you're winning.

 **Remember, it's just a game - unless you're streaming, in which case, panic!**

## Your leisurely walk will always include an unexpected downpour.

 **A pocket-sized poncho makes you look less surprised, more prepared.**

# ENTERTAINMENT AND LEISURE

The book spoiler will appear on your social media feed just before you finish.

 Adopt a no-scroll policy when nearing the end of a good read.

The concert tickets for your favorite band will sell out in seconds.

 Sometimes a live-stream is just as good, and you can control the volume.

## The vacation spot will be nothing like the brochure.

Lower your expectations; some of the best memories are made in "Plan B" moments.

# RELIGION AND SPIRITUALITY

You'll remember it's a fasting day after having breakfast.

 Post reminders where you'll see them first thing in the morning, like your bathroom mirror.

Your "short and sweet" prayers will always be interrupted by your phone.

 Silence the phone or place it in another room when engaging in spiritual activities.

# RELIGION AND SPIRITUALITY

The inspirational quote you share will have a typo only after it's too late.

 Proofread twice; post once.

You'll finally achieve deep meditative focus just as construction work starts in your neighborhood.

Use natural sounds in headphones to create your own tranquil inner world.

# RELIGION AND SPIRITUALITY

The hymn you don't know will be the one you're asked to lead.

 A smile can be a universal verse. Use it liberally.

You'll find spiritual enlightenment...right before the Wi-Fi cuts out during the online service.

 Consider it a sign to unplug more often.

**You'll remember to be grateful just when you're complaining.**

**Maintain a gratitude journal. It's harder to complain when you're aware of your blessings.**

# PETS AND ANIMALS

Your cat will only want to sit on you when you're allergic or wearing black.

 Always keep a lint roller handy and perhaps an antihistamine.

The dog will finally do the trick perfectly when no one is around to see it.

 Always have your phone camera ready. You never know.

# PETS AND ANIMALS

**Your fish tank will stay clear until the day you have guests.**

 **Invest in a reliable water filtration system—and a discreet net.**

**Birds will only sing loudly during your important video calls.**

 **Prep your "mute" button reflexes.**

# PETS AND ANIMALS

Your pet will find the most inconvenient places to hide - like when you're running late for the vet.

 Keep a list of your pet's favorite hiding spots. It's like a treasure map, but more frustrating.

Your pet will decide it loves your least favorite person the most.

Well, pets are great judges of character, but they also love treats. Check your friend's pockets.

**You will run out of poop bags only when your dog decides to go twice.**

 **Always carry extra. Always.**

# AUTOMOTIVE AND MECHANICS

Your car will only break down when you're in a rush.

 Regular maintenance can help prevent unexpected issues. Keep an emergency kit just in case.

Your "check engine" light will turn off as soon as you reach the mechanic.

 Take a video or photo when the light is on. Proof is in the pixels.

# AUTOMOTIVE AND MECHANICS

The radio will blast at max volume when you least expect it.

 Make it a habit to lower the volume before turning off your car.

The one tool you need is the one you can't find.

 Organize your tools. Label them if you must.

# AUTOMOTIVE AND MECHANICS

**A 10-minute oil change will inevitably take an hour.**

 **Always block off more time than you think you'll need for car repairs.**

**You'll wash your car today; it will rain tomorrow.**

 **Check the weather forecast before picking up that sponge.**

# AUTOMOTIVE AND MECHANICS

## The cup holder will be too small for your favorite travel mug.

 Test out cup sizes before you buy. Or buy a smaller favorite mug.

# SHOPPING AND CONSUMERISM

The item you want is always out of stock.

OUT OF STOCK

 Call ahead or check online inventory before you make the trip.

The fastest checkout line will become the slowest as soon as you join it.

 Patience is a virtue. Bring a book or prepare to people-watch.

# SHOPPING AND CONSUMERISM

Coupons expire
the day before you
remember to use
them.

 Use a coupon organizer or set
reminders on your phone.

You'll realize you
forgot an item the
moment you reach
the parking lot.

 Always double-check your list
before heading to the cashier.

# SHOPPING AND CONSUMERISM

The shopping cart will always have one squeaky, wobbly wheel.

 Give the cart a quick test drive before committing.

The "easy to open" packaging never is.

 Keep a box cutter or a good pair of scissors handy.

# SHOPPING AND CONSUMERISM

**Your favorite product will be discontinued.**

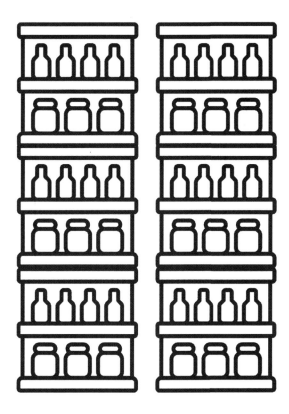

 **When you find something you love, consider stocking up.**

# COMMUNICATION AND MEDIA

**Your phone will ring at the most inconvenient time.**

 Use 'Do Not Disturb' or silent mode during important meetings or activities.

**The news will break important updates during your favorite show.**

 Record your favorite shows to watch later, so you don't miss anything.

# COMMUNICATION AND MEDIA

**Autocorrect will fail you when you most need it.**

Always proofread important messages before hitting 'send.'

**Your Internet will go out seconds before your work deadline.**

Save your work often and have a backup internet solution, like a mobile hotspot.

# COMMUNICATION AND MEDIA

Your email spam filter will catch important messages but not actual spam.

 Regularly check your spam folder and adjust the settings as needed.

Social media will show spoilers for the show you haven't watched yet.

 Mute or unfollow accounts that frequently post spoilers.

# COMMUNICATION AND MEDIA

**The moment you pay for a subscription, all your favorite content vanishes.**

 **Check the content library before committing to any service.**

# CONSTRUCTION AND DIY PROJECTS

The one tool you need is always missing.

 **Take inventory of your tools before starting a project.**

Your project will require at least three trips to the hardware store.

 **Always buy extra materials to save yourself another trip.**

# CONSTRUCTION AND DIY PROJECTS

Measurements will be off by just enough to ruin everything.

 Measure twice, cut once.

The 'easy assembly' project never is.

Read all instructions fully before starting. You might also want to look up video tutorials.

# CONSTRUCTION AND DIY PROJECTS

**You will finish painting only to discover you missed a spot.**

 **Always do a final walk-through before cleaning up your painting supplies.**

**Your DIY project will cost more than buying it pre-made.**

 **Budget generously and account for unexpected costs.**

# CONSTRUCTION AND DIY PROJECTS

**Your neighbors will decide to mow their lawn during your most delicate project phase.**

 **Notify neighbors of any major construction and plan around potential disruptions.**

# PSYCHOLOGY AND BEHAVIOR

**The person you least want to see will appear when you're at your worst.**

 **A quick confidence-boosting mantra can help you face any unexpected encounter.**

**Your most embarrassing moment will have the most witnesses.**

 **Own it; humor disarms awkward situations.**

# PSYCHOLOGY AND BEHAVIOR

**You'll remember the perfect witty comeback hours too late.**

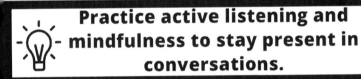

Practice active listening and mindfulness to stay present in conversations.

**You'll forget someone's name the instant they introduce themselves.**

Repeat the name back during the introduction to help it stick.

# PSYCHOLOGY AND BEHAVIOR

**Your inner critic is loudest when you need encouragement the most.**

 **Keep a list of past accomplishments to review when you need a boost.**

**You'll only realize you're overthinking when you've already lost sleep over it.**

 **Setting aside "worry time" earlier in the day can help you wind down before bed.**

**You'll think you're over an ex until you see them with someone else.**

 **Focus on your own growth and well-being; avoid stalking them on social media.**

# NATURE AND ENVIRONMENT

The moment you put away your umbrella, it will start to rain.

 Always carry a small, foldable umbrella when there's even a slight chance of rain.

Wildlife will only appear when you've put your camera away.

 Keep your camera on a sling for quick access.

# NATURE AND ENVIRONMENT

The mosquito will always bite the one spot you forgot to apply repellent.

 Use a mirror or ask someone to help you cover all areas with repellent.

The hiking trail will be clear until you wear your new white sneakers.

 Always wear appropriate and already broken-in footwear when going into nature.

# NATURE AND ENVIRONMENT

A 'beautiful day for a picnic' will turn windy the moment you spread the blanket.

 Bring some heavy items to weigh down corners of your blanket.

Your campfire skills will fail you when it's crucial to stay warm.

 Always carry fire starter kits and practice your skills before heading into the wilderness.

**The worst pollution is found in the most beautiful, remote areas.**

 **Always carry a bag to pick up trash, even if it's not yours.**

# FASHION AND PERSONAL CARE

**Your zipper will only break when you're running late.**

 **Always have a few safety pins on hand in case of a wardrobe malfunction.**

**You'll realize your clothes are inside-out after you've been out in public for hours.**

**A quick bathroom break can save you hours of embarrassment. Check yourself before you exit.**

# FASHION AND PERSONAL CARE

**Your new white shirt will attract spaghetti sauce like a magnet.**

 **Carry a portable stain remover pen for unexpected spills.**

**You'll find the other sock only after you've thrown its pair away.**

 **Keep a "lonely sock box" and check it every so often to make reunions.**

# FASHION AND PERSONAL CARE

The hairstyle you can never get right will be perfect right before bed.

 Document your steps when you do get it right. You'll be glad you did.

Your shaving razor will go dull when you're only halfway through shaving.

 Keep spare razors or a blade sharpener in the bathroom.

# FASHION AND PERSONAL CARE

## Your favorite perfume will get discontinued.

 **Once you find a scent you love, stock up.**

# SAFETY AND SECURITY

The fire drill will always occur when it's raining.

 Keep an umbrella in your office or desk for unexpected weather events.

The one day you forget your ID badge is the day security is on high alert.

 Keep a spare badge in your car or at home for such emergencies.

# SAFETY AND SECURITY

Your smoke detector's low-battery beep will only sound at 3 a.m.

 Schedule regular battery checks to avoid nocturnal surprises.

Your password will expire the day before a big presentation.

 Set a calendar reminder to update passwords before they expire.

# SAFETY AND SECURITY

The emergency exit will be used most frequently by people sneaking a smoke.

 Report misuse of safety exits; they should only be used in real emergencies.

The CCTV camera will malfunction precisely when you need it most.

 Regularly test all your security systems to ensure they're functional.

## The safety manual will be missing the page on the exact accident that occurs.

 Keep digital copies of safety manuals and protocols for easy access.

# ART AND CREATIVITY

Your most brilliant idea will come when you don't have a pen or paper.

 Keep a notepad and pen, or a note-taking app, handy at all times.

Your printer will run out of ink the moment you need to print your masterpiece.

 Always keep spare ink cartridges or know where to get a quick refill.

# ART AND CREATIVITY

The paint color that looked perfect in the store will look entirely different on your canvas.

 Test a small area before committing to a large-scale application.

Your favorite art supply store will discontinue your go-to product.

 Once you find a product you love, stock up!

# ART AND CREATIVITY

The moment you finish setting up your easel outdoors, it will start to rain.

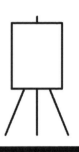

 Always check the weather forecast and be prepared with a backup plan.

Your best artwork will be the one you forgot to sign.

 Make signing your work the final step in your artistic process.

# ART AND CREATIVITY

You'll find the perfect spot for your painting after you've already put holes in another wall.

 Use removable hooks first to test locations before making it permanent.

# TIME MANAGEMENT AND PROCRASTINATION

The most important task will be the one you remember right before falling asleep.

 Keep a notebook by your bed to jot down these late-night thoughts.

You'll find every reason to clean your house when a deadline is looming.

Use a timer to limit your procrastination activities. When the timer goes off, it's back to work.

# TIME MANAGEMENT AND PROCRASTINATION

The simpler the task, the longer it will take due to unforeseen complications.

 Always allocate extra time for even the most straightforward tasks.

You will waste more time deciding which task to do first than actually doing any task.

 Prioritize tasks by deadline or importance, and stick to the list.

# TIME MANAGEMENT AND PROCRASTINATION

Your Wi-Fi will work flawlessly until you're on a tight deadline.

Have a backup plan like a mobile hotspot or a secondary workspace with reliable internet.

Inspiration strikes only when you're too busy to act on it.

Capture ideas in a note-taking app immediately, so you can revisit them later.

**Your focus will be sharpest five minutes before you need to leave.**

 **Plan short work sprints to capitalize on this burst of productivity.**

# SOCIAL MEDIA AND INTERNET CULTURE

The tweet you're most proud of will get zero likes, but a random retweet will go viral.

 Don't measure your worth by social media metrics; they're fickle.

You will stumble upon spoilers for your favorite show while avoiding work online.

 Use keyword filters to avoid spoilers on your social media platforms.

# SOCIAL MEDIA AND INTERNET CULTURE

Your phone will autocorrect to the most embarrassing typo when messaging someone you admire.

 Double-check your texts before hitting send, especially to someone significant.

The video you find hilarious will not be funny to anyone else you show it to.

 Enjoy your unique sense of humor; it's what makes you, you.

# SOCIAL MEDIA AND INTERNET CULTURE

You'll accidentally like an old photo while stalking someone's social media.

 Use a 'dummy' account for your stalking needs or scroll very, very carefully.

The time you set aside to work will be when all the interesting updates and memes appear.

 Use website blockers during your focused work time.

# SOCIAL MEDIA AND INTERNET CULTURE

You'll finally come up with a clever hashtag, only to find out it's already trending for something else.

#

 Do a quick search before finalizing your 'unique' hashtag.

# PHILOSOPHY AND ETHICS

The answer to life's biggest questions will come to you in the shower and be forgotten by the time you're dry.

 Keep a waterproof notepad in the shower for such eureka moments.

You will realize your moral high ground is shaky right after you've passionately defended it.

Before making bold statements, take some time to critically assess your viewpoints.

# PHILOSOPHY AND ETHICS

The philosopher you've ridiculed will be the only one covered in your final exam.

 It's wise to study all perspectives, even those you disagree with.

Your deep and thoughtful social media post will be overshadowed by a meme.

 Sometimes, simplicity wins the day. A concise message can be just as impactful.

# PHILOSOPHY AND ETHICS

You'll finally understand a complex theory - only to have it debunked the next day.

 Philosophy and ethics are ever-evolving. Keep an open mind.

In an ethical dilemma, all options will seem equally bad.

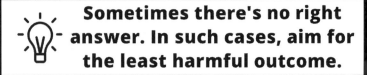 Sometimes there's no right answer. In such cases, aim for the least harmful outcome.

**Your most profound thoughts will occur at inconvenient times, like 3 a.m.**

**Keep a notebook by your bedside for late-night inspiration.**

The amount of time you spend on homework is inversely proportional to the grade you'll get.

 Consistent, focused study time will help you achieve better results.

The coolest clothing you own will inevitably be "so last week" when you wear it to school.

 Trends are fleeting. Aim for a timeless style.

Your phone's battery will die right when you're waiting for an important text.

 Always carry a portable charger.

Your crush will only notice you when you're having a bad hair day.

 Confidence is the best accessory.

The moment you claim to be "good at multitasking" is when you'll forget an important assignment.

 Use a planner to keep track of all your tasks.

✳ ✳ ✳ ✳ ✳

Your parents will always call you at the most inopportune times.

 Set boundaries and let them know when you're available to talk.

✳ ✳ ✳ ✳ ✳

When you finally have the perfect witty comeback, the argument will have moved on.

 Live in the moment. Not everything requires a comeback.

The day you sleep in is the day something significant happens in first period.

 Keep a consistent sleep schedule.

**Your favorite song will become annoying once it becomes your alarm tone.**

**Vary your alarm tones to keep them from becoming stale.**

**You'll understand a subject right after the test is over.**

**Preemptive studying and attending extra classes can work wonders.**

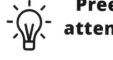

**Your hair will look perfect right before you shower.**

 **Document the moment; selfies are for good hair days.**

**You'll find the perfect pair of shoes, but they won't have your size.**

 **If shopping online, put them in your wishlist and check back frequently for restocks.**

# FOR WOMEN

The baby will wake up the moment you sit down to eat.

 Keep some quick snacks on hand for emergencies.

You will run into someone you know when you least expect- and want - to.

 Always have a pair of sunglasses and a hat for disguise.

# FOR WOMEN

Your nail polish will chip right after you've finished painting them.

 Use a good topcoat and avoid water for a few hours.

The day you forget your umbrella is the day it will rain.

 Keep a small portable umbrella in your bag at all times.

# FOR WOMEN

You'll get the most compliments on the outfit you like the least.

 Wear it when you have an obligatory event you're not thrilled about.

The recipe you decide to experiment with will fail when guests are over.

 Always have a quick backup meal idea.

# FOR WOMEN

**Your makeup will be flawless when you have nowhere to go.**

 **That's what social media is for—show it off!**

**You'll remember you ran out of tampons or pads at the least convenient time.**

 **Always keep a small stash in your purse for emergencies.**

# FOR MEN

The tools you need for a quick fix are always in the other toolbox.

 Keep a basic set of tools in multiple locations.

Your favorite sports team will start losing as soon as you begin watching.

 Record the game; maybe they'll win if they think you aren't watching.

# FOR MEN

The line you choose at the supermarket will inevitably be the slowest.

 Go for the line with the least number of people, not the least number of items.

You'll remember your wedding anniversary at midnight of the day after.

 Set multiple reminders. Trust me.

# FOR MEN

**Your hair will look best the day you're scheduled for a haircut.**

 **Learn some basic styling techniques for the "in-between" days.**

**The harder you try to impress someone, the more likely you are to spill your drink.**

 **Keep a napkin at hand and own any awkwardness with humor.**

# FOR MEN

The day you wash your car is the day it will rain.

 Always check the weather forecast before a car wash.

When you're in a rush, every red light in the city will conspire against you.

 Leave a little earlier than you think you need to.

# FOR MEN

## Your size will be the only one sold out.

 **If you find something that fits well, consider buying in multiple colors.**

## Your kids will need urgent attention only when you're in the middle of something important.

 **Keep some quick distractions on hand for such moments.**

You'll find the TV remote after you've gotten up to change the channel manually.

 Keep a designated spot for the remote.

The grandkids will call when you're in the middle of a nap.

 Set a "nap time" sign or status online to let them know the best times to call.

**You'll remember the perfect witty reply hours after the conversation ended.**

**Keep a journal of those gems for future use.**

**Your back will go out more than you do.**

**Regular exercise can help; consult your doctor for a suitable routine**

# FOR SENIORS

The pharmacy will be out of your prescription when you're on your last pill.

 Refill a week ahead of schedule if possible.

The book you're looking forward to will only be available in fine print.

 Consider an e-reader where you can adjust text size.

# FOR SENIORS

**Your favorite oldies station will start playing songs you consider "new music."**

 **Explore streaming services for specialized playlists.**

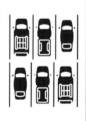 **You'll find the perfect parking spot after you've parked far away.**

 **Take the longer walk as an opportunity for some light exercise.**

You'll remember an important birthday or anniversary at 11:59 PM.

 Utilize digital reminders.

The item you need from the grocery store will be on the highest shelf.

 Don't hesitate to ask for help; store employees are there to assist.

Made in the USA
Middletown, DE
28 November 2023

43822872R00082